POWERFUL POSITIVE AFFIRMATIONS FOR WOMEN

ENCOURAGEMENT FROM THE HEART OF GOD

JENNIFER CARTER

Copyright © 2018 by Jennifer Carter

All rights reserved.

No part of this book may be reproduced in any form or by any electronic or mechanical means, including information storage and retrieval systems, without written permission from the author, except for the use of brief quotations in a book review.

Disclaimer and Terms of Use: The Author and Publisher has strived to be as accurate and complete as possible in the creation of this book, notwithstanding the fact that she does not warrant or represent at any time that the contents within are accurate. While all attempts have been made to verify information provided in this publication, the Author and Publisher assumes no responsibility for errors, omissions, or contrary interpretation of the subject matter herein.

Scriptures taken from the Holy Bible, New International Version ®NIV ®Copyright ©1973, 1978, 1984 by Biblical Inc.™ Used by permission of Zondervan. All rights reserved worldwide. www.zondervan.com

Scripture quotations from THE MESSAGE. Copyright © by Eugene H. Peterson 1993, 1994, 1995, 1996, 2000, 2001, 2002. Used by permission of Tyndale House Publishers, Inc.

Scripture quotations marked (NLT) are taken from the Holy Bible, New Living Translation, copyright ©1996, 2004, 2007, 2013 by Tyndale House Foundation. Used by permission of Tyndale House Publishers, Inc., Carol Stream, Illinois 60188. All rights reserved.

Scripture quotations taken from the New American Standard Bible®,

Copyright © 1960, 1962, 1963, 1968, 1971, 1972, 1973,1975, 1977, 1995 by The Lockman Foundation Used by permission. (www.Lockman.org)

INTRODUCTION

In the busyness of life, it can be all too easy to lose sight of the truth—the truth of who we are, as those chosen and loved by a Heavenly Father.

Despite having the best of intentions, we can struggle to find time to read the Bible and to learn and discover more about our true identity.

This book is for you if you simply need to be reminded of the truth and remember who you are.

It's for you if you're not sure who you are but want to find out more.

Discover what the Bible says about those who can call themselves children of God.

INTRODUCTION

The Bible, the Word of God, has the power to change lives.

Filled with truths from the Bible, these affirmations can help transform your mind and change your life.

You'll

- Read positive affirmations direct from the heart of your Heavenly Father.
- Hear what He says about you.
- Positive words.
- Hear words of encouragement and empowerment.
- Listen to words that can, quite literally, transform both your mind and heart.
- discover the power of the Word to change your thoughts, impact your thinking and your attitude.

Do you need an injection of biblical truth?

To hear that you are loved by a heavenly Father?

To understand how special and precious you are?

Reboot your life

Take a few moments to read or listen to these words of affirmation, drawn from the Bible, that speak about your true identity.

INTRODUCTION

Words that have power—power to transform your mind and encourage your heart.

Refresh and renew your mind with the powerful truths in the Word of God. Life-changing truths can help you overcome the lies of the enemy.

As you read through these transformative affirmations, it can help chase away the lies that have been spoken about you.

Allow these words from the Father to change your thinking, and help reaffirm your true identity in Christ.

Soak yourself in the Word of God.

Discover the supernatural blessings that are already yours.

Bathe your mind in the truths of what God says about you.

Let His love and truth transform you.

Let these truths strengthen and empower you.

Are you ready?

YOU ARE CHOSEN

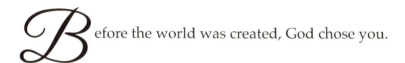efore the world was created, God chose you.

Before the foundations of the earth were laid, you were on God's mind.

He took pleasure in planning everything about you. Your adoption into His family. His plan to bring you freedom, abundant freedom. He works it all out. Everything. According to His purpose and His will.

Your Heavenly Father made you…out of nothing. From nothing, His hands formed you. He breathed life into you. He put you together perfectly. Nothing is out of place, and all is as it should be.

The Creator of the Universe made you and formed you.

You are wonderfully made—a masterpiece. Don't let anyone tell you otherwise.

Before you were born, while you were still in your mother's womb, He prepared the days of your life.

You were planned. By Him. Planned. Intended. Not an accident, a mistake, or a random happening. But planned by Almighty God and part of a perfect plan.

God planned you and has a purpose for you.

The Father speaks…He says, "You're mine." It's your Father who called you. He chose you as His child and set you apart from the beginning of time to be special—a child of your perfect Heavenly Father.

He knows what He's doing. It's all planned out. He promises

to take care of you. He won't leave you or abandon you. His plan is to give you a bright future.

So hold on to hope. Trust Him. Don't doubt His love. The Father has planned your future, and it's bright. He's working out everything according to the purpose of His will.

You are loved by God. He's adopted you into His family. You're His treasured possession, His precious adopted child, chosen by Him.

You're marked in Him with a seal by the Holy Spirit. This seal, the presence of the Holy Spirit, is the guarantee of your inheritance. Your inheritance as His child is sure.

And none of this was because of who you were or are.

For God chose the weak and foolish so that His glory could be displayed in you.

He took you from nothing and made you into something.

Once, you were rejected, but now you are fully accepted in Him.

Once, you were condemned, but now you are forgiven.

Once, you were dead because of wrongdoing, but He made you alive.

God's done it all through Jesus Christ.

God sent Him to lay down His life for you.

All through Jesus and His sacrifice.

You're chosen by God. Such love He has for you! What grace He has shown you. What incredible gifts He has freely given you. What a privilege to be called a child of the living God.

So don't let anyone sideline you or take you down the wrong path.

There's no need to fear or worry. The Father's called you by name. You're His. No-one can take you out of His hands.

As His child, you don't belong to this world; this isn't your real home.

The world may throw its worst at you, but God's promise to you stands firm.

Whatever deep waters you pass through, you won't drown. Whatever fire you pass through, you will not be overwhelmed. Whatever hotspot you're in, it won't consume you.

God, your very own Father, will rescue you because He delights in you. He wants to lavish His love on you.

His plan, His perfect plan is being worked out in your life. Each day, you're being transformed into His glorious likeness. One day, when He comes, you will be perfect, like Him.

It's in your make-up to be like Him. It's part of His plan.

He's placed eternity in your heart. One day He'll take you home to be with Him.

You're chosen, part of God's family. A royal family. Set apart. Holy. Special. Adopted. Forgiven. Loved.

YOU ARE DECLARED RIGHT WITH GOD

You have been made right with God. Sin has no hold on you.

Not so long ago, you were wading around in the filth of your sin, going your own way, being hateful and being hated. Your focus was on yourself. You were a prisoner living in a prison made of your own wrongdoing.

God sent Jesus, His Son, who was pure and holy, and put every wrong thing you ever did on Him. While you were still slumming it, Christ died for you.

You don't have to try to follow the impossible rules of 'do

this' or 'do that'. He's done it for you. He's set you free—free from being enslaved by passions and pleasures.

In His love for you, He sent Jesus. He's rescued you, removed the impossible barriers that stood in your way, and brought you in close to be friends with Him.

He did everything needed to set you free from sin. Everything He did, He did to bring you to God, the Father. Jesus died for you.

There's no more working your guts out to please God. However hard you try, you can't impress Him with your efforts. You're living a new life of faith in Jesus, God's Son, the One who conquered death once and for all. You can count on Him. Trust Him.

Jesus' sacrifice was enough. His light—His unapproachable and perfect light—cancels out the darkness that once was in you. Sin is powerless. It's hold over you is null and void.

The Father has taken your old filthy rags of sin and burnt them to ashes. He's dressed you in beautiful, clean robes. You're washed clean, both inside and out. He took you from the dust heap and made you new.

He's given you a gift, a gift of being made right with God.

You have a destiny, God's gift to you—eternal life in Christ Jesus.

So when the accusers point their finger and whisper behind your back, trust God. In the final count of your life, He'll declare you innocent of every charge made against you. No more condemnation. You're set free from sin.

When that messenger arrives at your door with a parcel of filth, hate, greed, and lust addressed to you, send him away. You don't need to live in that life anymore. You're free—so live as someone who is free rather than as a slave to your old life.

That old life was up there on the cross with Jesus. It's dealt with. Now you have a new life. You're fully alive, full of a life that's given by God.

Now you're living by faith. You've been declared right with God.

Listen to God. Hear His gentle whisper.

Focus on Him. Live for Him!

YOU ARE ADOPTED

*Y*ou're a child of God.

He's brought you into His family and welcomed you in. He's opened up His heart to you.

You have a new identity, a new family. You're part of His Kingdom.

Such love He has for you! Perfect love. Pure love.

He longs to lavish your weary heart with His love. He longs to pour out His Spirit on you and in you.

Yes, this Heavenly Father, who lives in unapproachable light, has brought you in as His child.

It brings Him such pleasure to have you, His precious child, in His family.

The One who was to be your judge, who had every right to condemn you, sets you free.

Not only that, but He becomes your Father.

You can call the creator of the universe your Father.

Your daddy. Papa. Dad.

Even when you run from Him, He's there, patiently waiting. He longs to run and embrace you when you return, to celebrate and party when you come back to Him.

You can't lose your identity, no matter how far or long you run from Him. You're His child. He's always looking out for you.

This adoption is powerful. You're part of His family forever. It's all signed and sealed in His name.

He's given you the right to use His name, a citizenship in heaven, and an inheritance.

He'll care for and provide for you. The rights that Jesus has as Son He's given to you.

You were once far away from the family of God, a slave, an outsider to understanding God's ways.

Now He's brought you in to be part of His people, with all the sons and daughters He's brought into this family.

He promises to be a Father to you and to them. There are no divisions between you. You're all one in Jesus.

He welcomes you into the courts of His presence. He longs to share His thoughts with you. To speak to you in a gentle whisper. To reveal His heart to you.

He promises He'll never leave you and never abandon you. He'll always be with you.

Everything He has is yours—it's all yours.

You're promised an incredible inheritance that is rich, abundant, and overflowing.

He's sent you His Spirit to remind you and confirm your true identity as His child. Allow God's Spirit to lead you.

You know that Jesus, because of the death He died, is crowned with glory and honour. It is this same Jesus, who is even now with the Father, who will unashamedly call you sister, brother.

So don't take any of this for granted. Don't let anyone lead you down the wrong path.

Live no longer as a slave but as a precious child adopted by the Father. Live as a child of God. You've been chosen by Him. Adopted by Him.

There will be times of hardship when God is teaching and training you, just as any father helps and teaches his child.

He does this *because* He loves you and wants the best for you. Your Father promises that the good things in the future will far outweigh your present difficulties.

The Father is righteous and sinless. He's the ruler. The eternal One. The King.

You're His adopted child—chosen. Holy. Beloved.

YOU ARE FORGIVEN

You're accepted. You're forgiven. Washed clean of every wrongdoing.

Fully forgiven.

You've been washed whiter than snow. Every wrong thing you've done or thought has been forgiven.

God, the Father, has made your spirit pure; He's cleansed your conscience.

At one time you were dead; you were on a path destined for

downfall. Your disobedience and offences separated you from God. You were destined for destruction.

While you were dead, God, the compassionate and gracious One, reached out to you. He helped you to decide "No more!", to change your mind and to desire a new course for your life.

It's His kindness and patience that led you to turn away from your wrongdoing, from holding on to things and habits that were offensive to Him.

He's turned your life around, is helping you start walking in the right direction.

You were dead, but He rescued you, saved you, and made you alive. Really alive.

He took your sins—those times when you'd missed the mark, those times when you'd wilfully disobeyed Him—and He's wiped them out.

Your slate is clean. Every foolish mistake has been blotted out. Obliterated. Completely gone.

Once, you were overwhelmed by your offences, but the Father has taken them and thrown them into the deepest ocean.

He's forgiven everything—it's all wiped out. He's purified you and washed your guilty conscience away. To cap it all, He's said He won't remember your sins or hold them against you.

Instead of treating you as you deserved, He rescued you. He's given you a new heart and a new spirit. He promised that you, who were once far away from God, will receive the gift of the Holy Spirit. His Spirit.

Instead of crushing you, He brings you joy and contentment. Instead of the death you deserved, He gives you the precious gift of eternal life.

And there's no boasting. You can't work your way into this gift. You can't attain it by your puny efforts. It's a generous gift to you—you who deserve nothing—from your Heavenly Father.

God paid the highest price for your freedom. His Son, Jesus Christ, cleared the way for you. He was abandoned, disowned by God, so that you could be forgiven.

Condemned, crushed, and crucified so that you could be accepted. Raised to life so that you could be set free.

You deserved to be condemned and punished, but He took the punishment that you deserved. He took all God's anger. He took it all on Himself in order that you might live free.

He's torn down the barriers between you. Now you can walk right up to God, boldly, to say whatever you need to say.

As you turn from your wrongdoings, He'll restore you and give you times of refreshing.

So trust in Him, and put your faith in Jesus. Believe in what He's done for you. All this blessing is because of His great love and compassion. It's nothing that you've done.

Once you were guilty, but now the only Holy and righteous judge has acquitted you.

He's the faithful one, and He always does what is right.

He's taken your punishment and revoked your licence to sin.

He's cleaned you up, and He's on your case.

So turn to Him. Trust Him. Respect Him. Honour Him.

Call on His name. Put your hope in Him. Come right up close to Him.

Get rid of anything that gets in between you and Him.

Forgive. Forgive again and again. Keep forgiving.

Do those things that you did at first when you first heard Him call you.

Remember that your life counts for something.

So live!

Live as a child of the light.

Live as one who has been purchased at a great price.

You are forgiven.

Live free!

YOU ARE SET APART

From the first moment you put your trust in Jesus, you were washed clean.

You were set apart. Made holy.

Your own efforts couldn't clean you up.

Nothing you tried worked.

But God chose you before the creation of the world.

When you trusted in Jesus, you were washed, cleansed and purified. Set free from sin.

You're part of God's family, special and dearly loved.

Holy and without blame in His eyes.

When you believed, God marked you with a seal.

He filled you with the Holy Spirit, the One He promised to send.

His Spirit dwells in you, your body now a temple.

This Spirit guarantees God's promises and your eternal security.

You've been given a fresh start.

You're no longer your own but part of God's chosen people.

He's called you to a new life.

You're to live by God's standards, distinct from the world.

So keep being filled with the Spirit.

Bear with each other. Exercise self-control.

Flee from foolish and harmful desires.

Pursue what is true, honest, pure, lovely, and just.

Delight in excellence and anything that's truly worthy of praise.

Embrace compassion. Be gentle.

Learn patience. Walk humbly.

Trust God with your money, and be generous.

Don't be ensnared by temptation.

Stop wasting your time.

Bear with each other.

Forgive one another.

Remember how God forgave you.

Train yourself to be godly.

Give thanks.

Offer yourself, your cleansed self, to God. This is real, honest worship.

Be holy in the way you live.

Be even tempered and full of quiet strength.

Let Christ be your all in all.

The Father's transforming you, making you like Jesus.

He's set you apart.

He'll cleanse you, through and through, again and again.

Living His way will bring you true, deep satisfaction.

Open your eyes to the incredible inheritance that God has called you to, all that you have in His kingdom.

Understand the amazing love of Christ—it's wider, longer, and deeper than you can possibly conceive.

YOU ARE SET FREE

*Y*ou've been set free.

Free from sin.

Free from fear.

Free from the enemy who held and bound you.

You're no longer a prisoner.

Once, you were a slave. A slave to your passions and desires.

You lived in despair. Held fast by the law of sin and death.

Without hope, you needed someone to rescue you from your prison—that dark dungeon where you were held captive.

God's love, His Spirit, His life, set you free.

Once, you lived as a slave, controlled and led by your passions and life's pleasures.

All of your life you were held in captivity.

You lived with envy and hate.

You were trapped—overcome by the corruption of your heart.

You'd lost hope and were sunk in the deepest pit of despair.

The One who overcomes set you free.

He's the rescuer, and He released you.

He has overcome all the sins that threaten to overtake and overwhelm you.

He's greater than the enemy that you face in this world.

Your old, sinful self was nailed to the cross with Jesus.

The highest price was paid for you.

Your enslavement was broken, once for all time.

You finally came to your senses and escaped from the trap you were in.

Sin was what you were called out of—freedom is what you were called in to.

Your sin put you on the pathway to death, but God's gift has set you on the pathway to eternal life.

His covenant, His promise to you is that…

He's replaced that fear with love and with Holy Spirit power…with liberty of mind and spirit.

Instead of foolishness, He's given you good judgement.

You're known by God, loved by Him.

You no longer are subject to bondage.

No longer a prisoner of your desires.

No longer subject to the whims and mercies of your passions

No longer destined to live as a slave.

Through Him, you are an overcomer.

As you bathe in His truth, He'll lead you victorious.

His truth brings freedom, breaks every shackle.

Nothing can hold you down.

God always has the last word.

Your Father listens when you call.

He answers you.

He will be with you in times of trouble.

He will rescue and deliver you.

He'll do it all because He delights in you.

He loves you.

He's released you from the prison of sin.

Broken the power of death.

Conquered fear.

His truth is victorious.

The old ways have no right over you.

That life is dead, over.

Your conscience is clear.

Uncontaminated.

You have a new life.

Longing to please the Father.

Longing to do things His way.

Because of Him, you live as one who is free.

Really free.

Through Him, you're fully alive.

Alive to God and open to Him.

Even though those around you still live as slaves, you've been given a promise, a hope.

You've received this through putting your complete trust and confidence in Jesus.

Your hope is in Him.

He's set you free and given you life.

Abundant life.

YOU ARE VICTORIOUS

God is for you.

Who can be against you?

Through Jesus, He's given you the victory.

Victory over sin and death.

Victory over the enemy of your soul.

He'll crush the enemy under your feet.

Nothing can separate you from God's love.

He'll never forsake you.

He's with you now.

He'll never leave you.

God, your God, will help you.

He watches over you.

Call on Him.

He's near to you.

He'll answer you.

He'll rescue you.

Protect you.

Uphold you.

Those who threaten you will be defeated.

Those you struggle with will disappear.

Those you fight will be made as nothing.

So don't be afraid. He'll help you.

Let Him fight this battle.

Put your faith in Him.

Trust Him.

Call on Him.

Take refuge in Him.

Hold fast to Him.

He'll strengthen you and help you.

Stand tall.

Stand your ground.

You can win this battle.

With Him, you'll overcome.

He'll crush the enemies you face.

You're led by the Lion of Judah.

The King of Kings.

Jesus, the Son of God.

The victory belongs to Him.

He delights in rescuing you.

In leading you to victory.

He's faithful.

He'll help you stand up when you face temptation.

He loves you.

Always.

Forever.

He'll never back out on His promises.

Be strong.

Have courage.

Stand. Stand firm.

See how He'll rescue you.

Pray.

Whatever happens…pray.

Bring every request to Him.

Push through.

Persevere.

Don't give up.

Keep asking Him.

Be strong in His mighty power.

The power that raised Jesus from death now lives in you.

That power is greater than you can imagine.

Incredible.

Put your faith in Him.

Get right before Him.

Live with integrity.

Be blameless, honest, and upright.

Trust His Word.

Respect His laws.

Believe His promises.

Put your hope in Him.

Delight in Him.

He'll lead you to victory.

Rejoice in how He saves you.

You're a child of the living God.

The precious child of a Heavenly Father.

BECOMING A CHRIST-FOLLOWER

*A*s you've been reading through these beautiful words, have you wondered if they apply to you?

Are you doubtful that these beautiful truths could be spoken about you?

Would you like to be part of the family of God so that you can know these truths and embrace them as your own?

Would you like to be sure, really sure, just who you really are?

The Bible says:

"For God so loved the world, that he gave his only Son, that

whoever believes in him should not perish but have eternal life. For God did not send his Son into the world to condemn the world, but in order that the world might be saved through him." (John 3:16–17, NIV)

The Father sent the Son, Jesus, to rescue you—to bring you into the family of God.

Are you ready to make a choice to follow Jesus Christ?

You can join God's family by praying this simple prayer:

Father,

I am sorry for things I have done wrong.

Thank you that Jesus died for me, rose from the dead, and is alive today.

Please forgive me for living life my own way.

Please come into my life and fill me with your Holy Spirit.

I accept Jesus Christ as my Lord and Saviour.

I choose to follow Him today and every day.

Amen

If you've prayed this prayer from your heart, you are forgiven. All the wrong things you have ever done have been taken away.

You're now a child of God and are starting a new life, an eternal life strengthened by the power of the Holy Spirit.

You have a new identity as a child of God. Every promise spoken in this book applies to you.

Read or listen again, and allow these truths to soak into your mind and heart.

What Do I Do Now?

Tell someone! If you know other Christ-followers, tell one of them that you have prayed this prayer.

Find and read your Bible. If you don't have one, get a hold of one.

Get involved in a local church. A good church will help you to grow and learn as a Christ-follower.

Pray. Talk to God, thank Him for the good things, forgive others, and ask Him for your daily needs.

ONE MORE THING

If you've enjoyed this book, it'd be great if you'd consider leaving a review, which helps other people to find it.

Thank you.

ABOUT THE AUTHOR

Jennifer Carter is a child of God.

She's someone who's taken the wrong path but has been saved by God's goodness and grace, rescued by His love and compassion.

She believes that the Bible, the Word of God, has the power to change lives.

You can see her latest books at www.jennifer-carter.com.

You can find her on Facebook, www.facebook.com/JenniferCarterWriter/

OTHER BOOKS FROM JENNIFER CARTER

Women of Courage - explore the lives of inspiring women from the Bible, through thirty-one daily bible readings.

Daily Readings for Difficult Days - a daily devotional for Christian women going through difficult times, including divorce, death of a loved one, depression and other struggles.

Experience Easter - based on the events leading up to the crucifixion. These twenty-six devotions look at real lives, of the men and women close to Jesus, and the meaning of Easter for us today.

Books for Children

A Christmas Surprise - read-aloud stories (for ages 3-6) look at the real Christmas story by those who saw it.

Made in the USA
Middletown, DE
15 May 2019